Racing pige

CONTENTS

Keeping racing pigeons

Racing pigeon (homing pigeon)

Lots of people keep racing pigeons.
People who own racing pigeons join clubs.
The clubs hold races for the pigeons.

Racing pigeons can always find their way home.
In some races, home is a long way away.

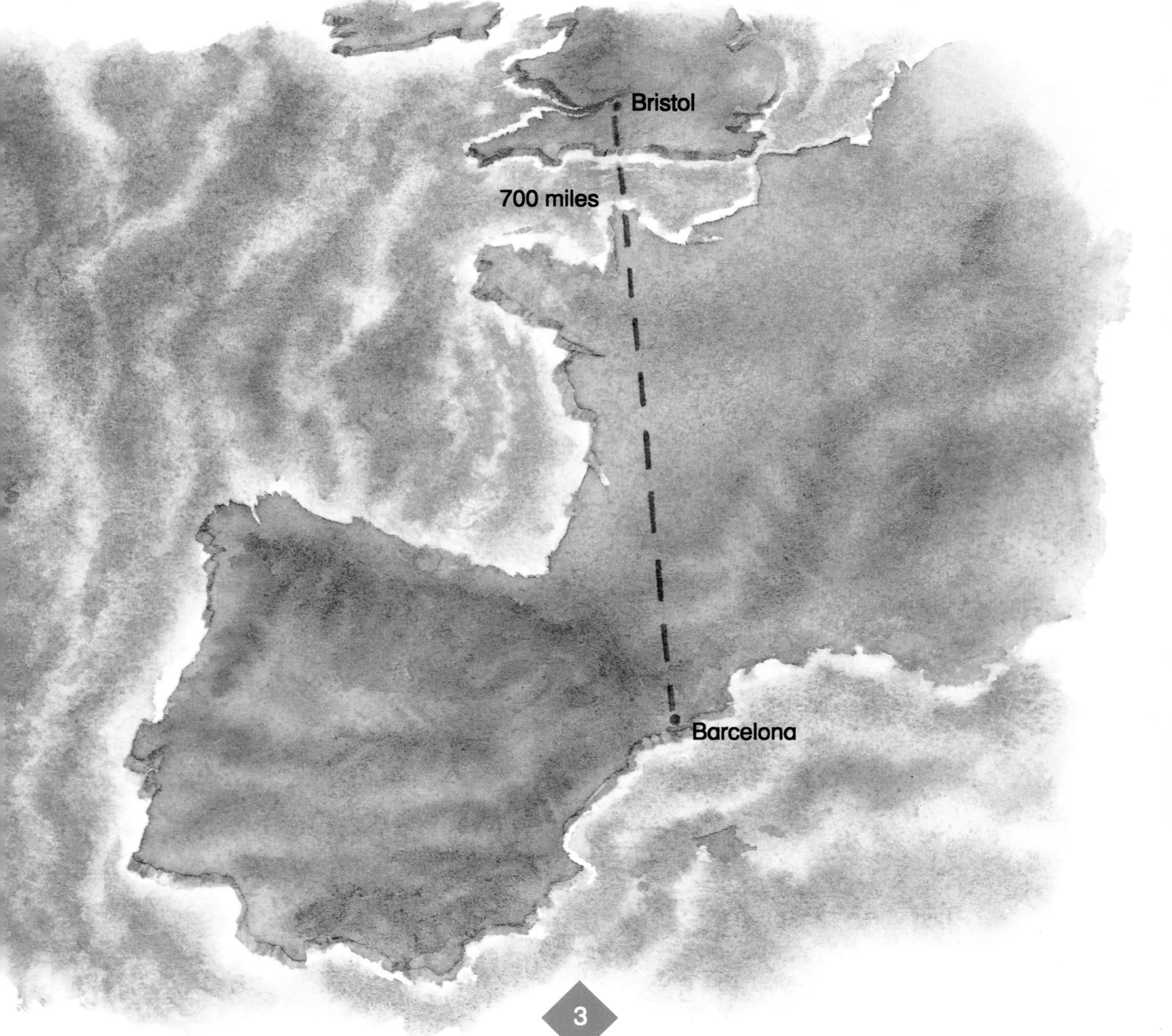

Jo's pigeons

Jo and her dad keep racing pigeons in their garden. The birds live in pigeon lofts. Jo and her dad made the lofts.

Baby birds are called 'squeakers'.
They have a lot to learn.

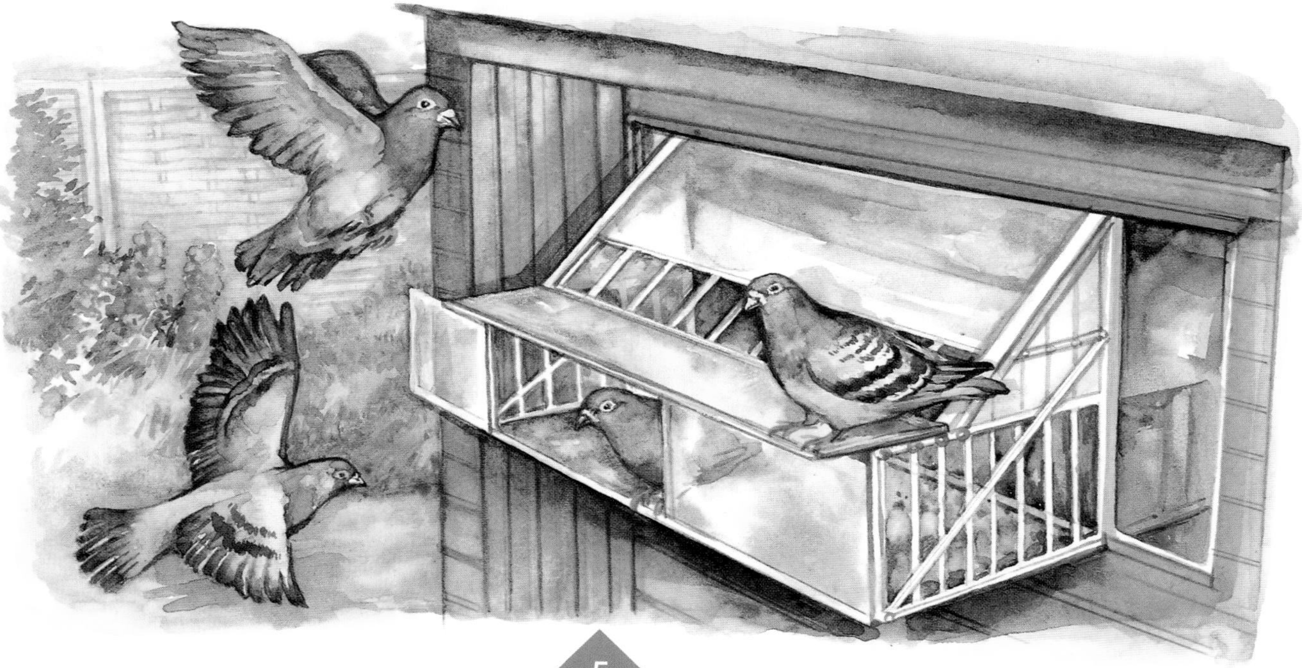

Jo whistles at feeding time.
The birds learn to come for food.

The garden is dangerous for baby birds.
They can only come out when Jo is there.
She makes sure other animals don't catch the birds.

Jo and her dad train the birds to fly home.

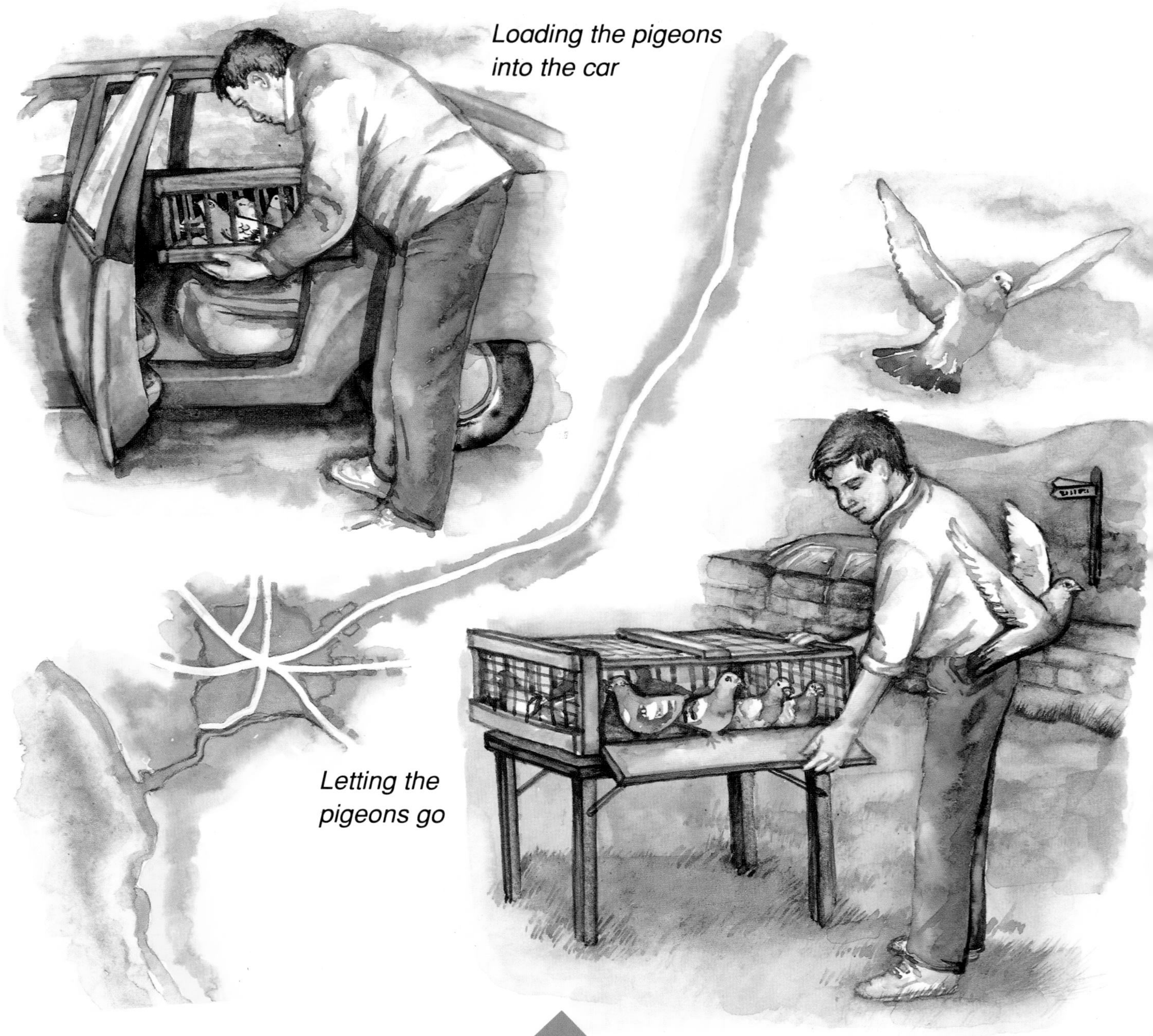

Loading the pigeons into the car

Letting the pigeons go

Waiting for the pigeons to fly home

Helping the pigeons into the loft

The race

Today is the first race of the year.
Jo takes ten birds to the club.
Jo's best bird is Blade.

Getting the birds ready for the race

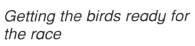

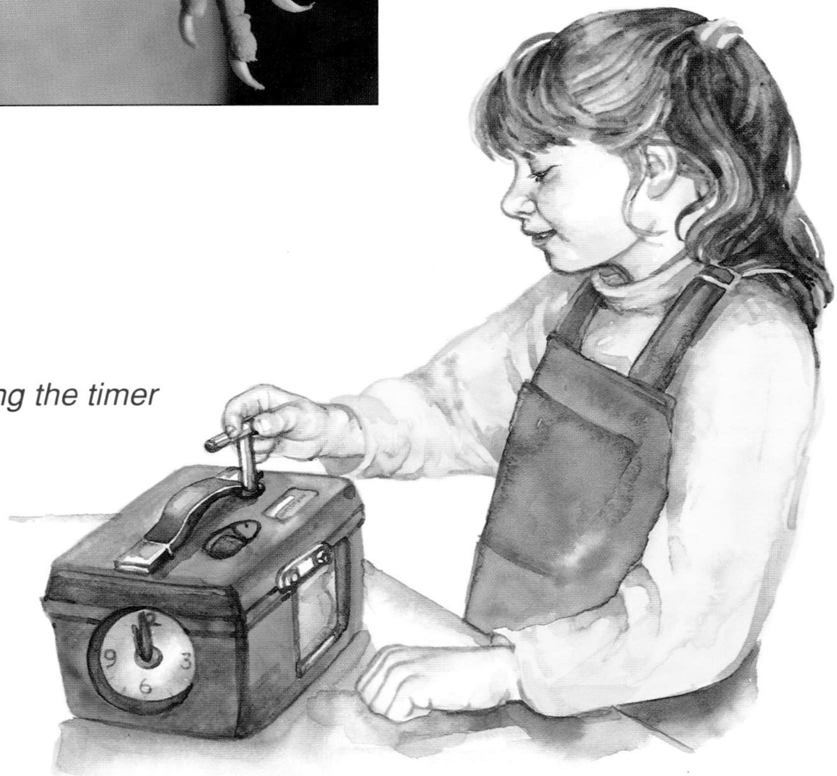

Setting the timer

The pigeons are put on a lorry.

Jo goes home. She hopes it will be sunny for the race.

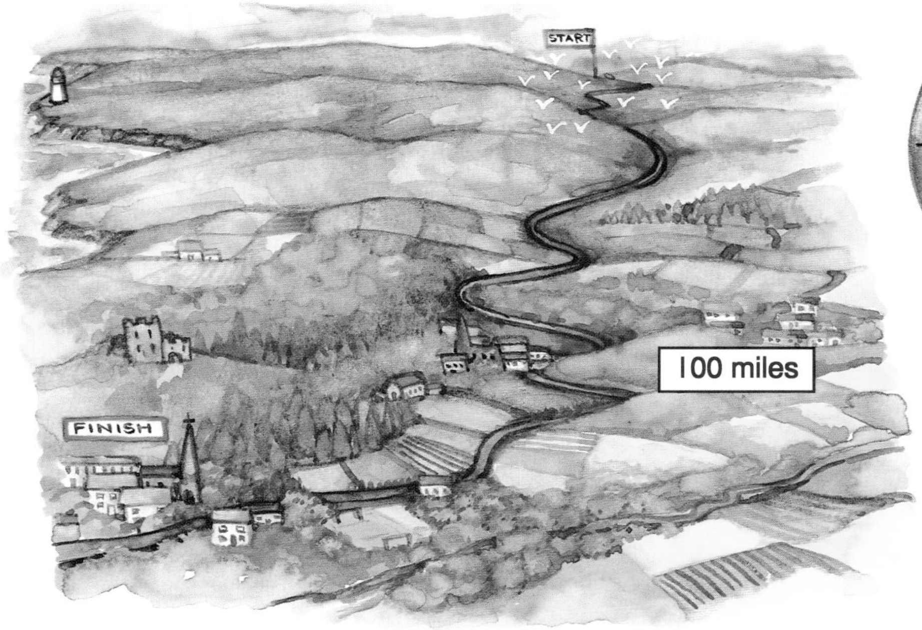

The lorry takes the pigeons to the start of the race.

The lorry driver opens the crates and the pigeons fly out.

Jo waits in the garden.
She watches the pigeons
coming back. Blade comes
back first.

Timing how long the pigeons took to fly home

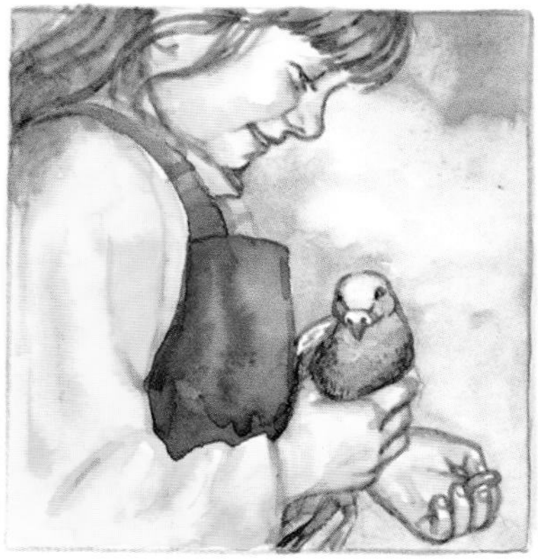

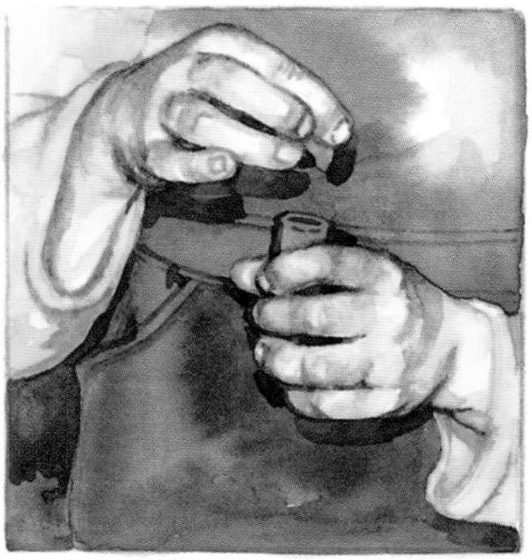

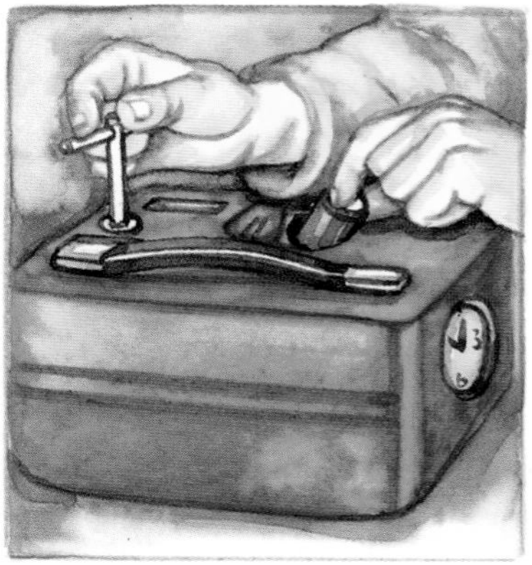

All the birds are back safely. Jo goes to the club. Blade is second and gets a prize. Jo is thrilled.

Index